The Mistakes of a Man

M. SOSA

Bestselling author of
The Mistakes of a Woman

First Print, November 2018

ISBN: 978-0-9951533-7-0

"It takes a *real* man to realize he's messed up and a *better one* to try to fix it."

- M. Sosa

Chapters

Introduction

The scenarios in this book are based on interviews done with 202 men. They were asked 45 questions each where they shared their past experiences and also shared parts of their personal lives.

To the men, I hope this book encourages you to learn more about a woman's emotional and physical needs. It is written from a woman's perspective. This was not written to insult or degrade men nor women. The gender dynamic outlined in this book is reversible.

CHAPTER 1
Hiding your feelings

"Women aren't the only
ones who build walls up.
Men just hide them better."

- M. Sosa

Growing up, we're told by our parents to express our feelings and to tell the truth when something bothers us, but we fail to realize that not all men and women were raised the same way.

I recall blaming my exes when they wouldn't express how they were feeling. I wanted to know why they were hurting or how I could fix their problems. The motherly instinct in me would kick in and all I wanted to do was save them from themselves. But instead of opening up, most of my exes hid behind an unbreakable wall. The harder I pushed, the more tension it caused between us. It's as if certain men were conditioned their whole lives to not talk about their feelings, or maybe they felt it was taboo.

That's when I understood that men and women hid their feelings for different reasons. For most women, crying or showing emotion comes naturally but for men, it's considered a sign of weakness. They're afraid that if they show any need for help that they'll be ridiculed or will be perceived as helpless, and that can be a significant hit to the ego for some.

Unfortunately, for us women, while we are eager to help and hear them out, we believe men are the same as us, so we expect them to dish out what they're feeling because that's what we would usually do.

Most women are able to easily express their frustrations when something's bothering them or when something doesn't seem right. Because of this, we expect our men to do the same.

Reality check—men won't always tell you what they're feeling. They prefer to be left alone to deal with things on their own. While you're trying to be an amazing partner, they're thinking of ways to get out from speaking about how they feel. It's not your fault.

What men fail to realize is that not opening up about how they truly feel can cause a lot of tension and misunderstandings in a relationship. Not sharing your emotions can make your partner feel as if you're losing your connection to one another. It can also make her feel as though you're withdrawn, and you don't care about how she feels. Even the idea of you leaving her can cross her mind.

Men haven't had the opportunity to open up to others, as easily as women have. Most women are able to meet up with girlfriends and talk about their issues while having dinner, having drinks or just kicking it. Men on the other hand aren't always able to express themselves without being judged by other males. Is it because they're scared of being vulnerable in front of them? Yes. That's why they end up hiding their true feelings because the last thing they want is to be perceived as weak.

Men express their feelings in things they feel comfortable with, in other words, anything that is considered "acceptable" or "safe". For example, look at how some men react when they speak about sports. They can go and on for hours about this player and that player, and what that player's strengths and weaknesses are. Notice how comfortable and how easily they express their feelings with one another during a football or basketball game. But if you were to place these same men in a different situation where they have to express their emotions to their partner, they might have a harder time doing so. That level of openness wouldn't be the same.

From my own observations, men experience overpowering emotions that sometimes make them put their guard up higher than before. They bury those emotions deeper and deeper because they don't know how to deal with them or lack the necessary support on how to make sense of them. This causes a problem for their partners because they feel they aren't able to help them, which sometimes lead to breakups or divorce. The fact that they've silenced their feelings for such a long period of time creates bigger issues because they're unsure how to handle them when they need to express them to their partners.

Even though society encourages men to express how they feel, it's not always easy for some because they're unsure how their partner will react to them. As much as we want men to open up to us, we're not always capable of handling what they say. To be honest, some men are horrified to tell us the because they're afraid we'll react abnormally.

Imagine having a man that's always poised and confident, and all of a sudden start breaking down crying in front of you. What would your first reaction be? While some of us would wonder what's going on, others will think their man is weak and he'll get over it on his own. That's the thing right there, because we're not used to seeing our man expressing any form of emotions, we sometimes believe they don't have any, but that's nothing further from the truth.

Men have feelings, they just hide them better. You've got to understand that unforeseen emotions can sometimes be overwhelming for a man, especially if he's not used to expressing how he feels. Be patient and listen to him, the same way you would expect him to listen to you.

I remember feeling this way with one of my exes. I felt he was withdrawn and closed up when it came to expressing what he was bottling in. As much as I pushed, he wouldn't budge. He just kept telling me that everything was okay, even though his mannerisms showed otherwise. A part of me felt as though I had done something wrong, but the reality was, he just didn't know how to say what he wanted to say. Expressing himself wasn't his strong point so I knew that no matter how much I pushed, he wouldn't feel comfortable telling me what was on his mind. This is when I realized that getting a man to open up was going to be one of the hardest things to do but if I succeeded, it would also be a great accomplishment on both sides.

Certain men believe that opening up to someone

is a huge risk because they're uncertain how the other person will perceive them afterwards. But if you don't try, how will you know? Everybody takes chances in life and being honest and open with your partner is a huge step towards learning from one another. It's not easy to let go of insecurities. It's pretty frightening but being able to communicate clearly what's bothering you or what's going on in your life is a great stress-reliever. You have no idea how amazing it is to speak your mind and tell others what's going through your head. I'm not telling you to let it all out one shot. On the contrary, take as much time as you need but know that the more you let out, the easier you'll find it next time to express your emotions.

Don't be the type of man that chases money to try to cover up his emotions either. While you may feel that buying yourself in your work will help you ignore those underlying feelings of anger or helplessness. Money will only be a temporary band-aid to hide the pain you're really feeling. Let it out.

The reason why women are so emotional is because we're able to feel the pain and feel it fully. We let that pain take over us to the point where we sometimes feel we're unable to fully function. But the beauty in all of it is knowing that no matter how much pain we're in, we're not hiding from it. We're letting others know what's hurting us or what made us feel that way. Men, on the other hand, will keep those emotions in until they're blue in the face. But the pain stays within in them until they decide they've had enough and want to let it all out.

CHAPTER 2
Being oblivious to how she feels

"If I would have *listened*…
If I would have *tried*…
If I would have *cared* a little more…
maybe you wouldn't have walked away."

- M. Sosa

<u>Men, please take note and read this carefully.</u>
Women are emotional and fierce individuals. We can't always shrug off what's bothering us or take things lightly. While you may be able to get over things faster than her, does not mean you should expect her to do the same. Whatever you do, don't try to control her feelings.

The worst thing you can do is be oblivious to how she's feeling. If something is bothering her, let her vent, listen and talk it through. Be sensitive to what she's going through. I'm not telling you to cater to her every need but it's important, in any relationship, to talk things through. Show empathy. Every relationship will go through its ups and downs but the moment you stop ignoring how she's feeling, you'll start making her feel as if you don't care.

Communicate your feelings to one another. The ability to share someone else's feeling is sacred and important if you want your relationship to grow. While women are known to be better at that than men, it doesn't mean you can't make the effort to try to understand what she's going through. Women want their feelings to be validated but they also want you to understand what their feelings are all about.

If there's one thing that will piss a woman off is a man that doesn't validate how their woman is feeling. It's one thing to nod your head while your woman is talking and pretending, you're listening to every word that's coming out of her mouth, all the while, you're thinking of who won the basketball game. You're not listening. You're pretending to listen. Know the difference and don't make the mistake of being one of those men.

A woman is usually ready to talk things out, but she also expects you to diligently engage in the conversation. She wants to feel assured that you're paying attention and that you're listening to whatever she's going through. The last thing she wants is a "yes" man that agrees to everything she says. She expects you to feel what she's feeling without making her feel as if she's begging for your attention. Some men will even go as far as pretending they're listening and cut the convo off by seducing their women with sex.

That's not the right strategy, gentlemen! While seducing your woman is a great idea, doing it while she is trying to make you feel what she's going through isn't the right approach because her feelings will only be covered up for a while

and will end up resurfacing when you least expect
it.

When you demonstrate an interest in what she's
saying, and you care enough to experience it
emotionally with her, you show her that you're
proactively trying to put yourself in her shoes. Be
sensitive, it doesn't take much.

Now, I can't put all the blame on men here
because as a woman myself, I realize there were
several times where I expected my ex to pick up
on my nonverbal signals instead of telling him
how I felt. This caused a lot of arguments because
I felt that he didn't understand me, or just didn't
care. But the reality was, he wasn't psychic and
couldn't always tell what I was feeling by little
signs. What was obvious to me wasn't always
obvious to him. I would have been better at
playing Poker and keeping a straight face than
hoping that he would see that something was
going on with me. If there's one thing I've
learned growing up is that you can't always shed
blame on your partner when you know you
weren't fully communicating either.

Many relationships end because they feel their
partner isn't showing empathy towards what
they're going through. There is no point dancing

around the truth and it's better to be honest and communicate your frustrations with one another instead of hiding them and expecting your partner to guess what they are. Be a fucking adult, you're not a child!

You see men aren't taught at an early age to pay attention to empathy. Men are taught to be strong and to not cry but aren't always given the basics when it comes to understanding what someone else is feeling. Because of this, men don't always see things from someone else's point of view and focus on what's in front of them instead. This causes men to not realize when their partner is upset or hurt because they assume their partner will tell them instead of sugarcoating it.

Now, gentlemen, when a woman tells you "I'm fine", most of the time–she isn't. Ask questions. Ask what you can do to make things better or how you can help. Don't just let things go. Do the work and don't fall into the same trap other men have fallen into. I'm not telling you to run after her and beg to know what's happening in her head but make the necessary effort to "try" to understand where the problem is coming from.
You see as much as I'd like to admit that I've never played that game of telling my partner that

I'm okay when I'm really not, I can't. I'm guilty for avoiding hard conversations because I was always unsure how my partner would react or if he would simply "get me". I wanted someone who would actively engage in the conversation and wouldn't just pat me on the shoulder and call it a day. And I think that's where most men mess up in general. You assume you can fix her problem by just telling her that things will be okay instead of actually feeling compassion for her needs.

Stop being an "oblivious and insensitive" man. It's time to learn empathy and learn how to read other people's feelings. You can't expect people's emotions to always be transparent. Things aren't always black and white and may take effort for you to realize that situations aren't as obvious as they seem.

A little bit goes a long way which means that you have to take the time to decipher what some people are throwing at you. Nobody is asking you to become a psychic but there are situations that shouldn't be ignored. I've seen men ignore women's advances because they were oblivious at the fact that the woman was hitting on them. Men won't always pick up on cues or make assumptions because they figure it's not about them… when it actually is.

Women on the other hand notice those subtle hunches and realize when something is off… call it a woman's intuition. As a man, you should make the same efforts and realize when someone is concerned, frustrated or even in need to talk.

Women want someone who's going to be present and will care about how she feels. If you're not planning on making that effort to notice these things, maybe that relationship isn't for you.

Put down your phone. Stop watching your basketball game. She wants to feel your presence which include your attention and connection. If there's one thing I can assure you it's that eventually that woman you love dearly will get fed up and you'll end up losing her over something you could've fixed if you had just taken the time. Remember, if you can't understand her, while she expects you to be her rock, you'll eventually push her further and further away.

Your role as her man is to know what makes her tick, what are her goals, what are her dreams. The same way she's always interested in knowing how you're feeling should be the same way you should be invested in knowing when something is on her mind.

CHAPTER 3
You're intimidated by her

"A powerful, independent woman will show you she doesn't need you to take charge because she's confident enough to do it *on her own*."

- M. Sosa

Being a man does not mean being in charge. Some of you might say this is farfetched and that you've never been intimidated by a woman. Yet, the majority of men I interviewed admitted otherwise after several open dialogues.

A powerful, independent woman is well-known in today's society. It's highly talked about over social media, the news, through music and TV, so there is no going around it. A woman with a tremendous amount of confidence can sometimes be intimidating while others may find it a major turn-on.

Certain men can't handle a woman with such high standards, and they'll end up doing whatever it takes to belittle them in hopes that they'll "bow down". That is the biggest mistake you can make towards a powerful woman because she will laugh in your face and will walk out that door the minute you start acting up.

A man that feels that his woman is overpowering him doesn't know how to act because he's not accustomed to being in second place. What some men fail to see is that the woman isn't trying to take charge and isn't trying to place herself above you, she's simply showing you that she's not scared to let you know what she's feeling and is fully capable of letting you know her dos and don'ts.

She doesn't need you to pick up the pieces of her life because she's constantly working on them. And I guess that's what causes the biggest confusion. Men don't know how to act when a woman doesn't actually need him.

You see a man's role in general is to protect and provide for his family. When you take one of those out of the equation, some men get lost and aren't sure how to handle you. And that's happened to me on several occasions because some of the men I dated couldn't understand why I didn't need them in the ways they were used to providing for other women.

I used to think I was the problem until I realized that the men, I dated were never comfortable with me being able to express myself. They thought I was too much while barely giving me a minimal amount of love. They thought I was the type of woman that would do everything they wanted without having a say in it but that's where they went wrong because I learned at an early age to speak my mind, and to stand strong with my beliefs. The men I dated weren't raised that way and believed I was the issue while not realizing they were the problem all along.

And you see, that's the thing, why are you scared of a woman that knows what she wants just because you're unsure of what you want? You should be proud that your woman is comfortable in her own skin. You should be proud that she is fierce and isn't afraid to show it. You should be proud that she doesn't need to put up with the head games either. But I think most of all, you should be proud that she's being herself and isn't trying to portray someone she isn't.

I think the one thing that scared my exes was the fact that I didn't need them to be myself. I felt accomplished and fulfilled because I knew I had built everything on my own without the help of anyone. And if they were looking to be my superhero, well I was already Superwoman, so that wouldn't work out quite well. You see, as much as I loved to share my life with them, that didn't mean that I was about to stop being ambitious and driven... and I think that's something they couldn't handle. You know that saying "They want to see you do good, but never better than them", well that's how they were.

Certain men can't handle a woman that exudes confidence or a woman that puts her dreams first. Why you may ask? It's simple, sometimes they're not at the same level as her and it makes them feel weak and uncomfortable. But you shouldn't feel this way because a woman that truly loves you and expresses that type of confidence usually wants you to be a part of her life, as long as you're there to respect and support her in everything she does too.

She might not need your help but that doesn't mean she doesn't want you to be a part of what she has going. Her standards are high and no matter what you do, she won't lower them anytime soon. So, if you want her in your life, either you suck it up and accept that she is who she is or walk away now and let her be great.

You can't stop a woman that knows what she wants but you can make the effort to be supportive and understand where she's headed. It's not a competition. You're supposed to be supporting one another, not competing against each other.

CHAPTER 4
Stop being possessive.
It's not cute.

"Growing together doesn't mean becoming possessive. What's mine is yours, and what's yours is mine but *my space is my space*. Don't try to control me."

- M. Sosa

Even though this book is geared towards men, I hope whomever is reading this will realize that these are traits found in both genders. Statistics show that men are more inclined to act this way but *if you see yourself in any of these examples, it may be time for you to seek some help.*

If you want to lose your woman's respect, treat her like a toy, a possession. There's nothing more annoying than trying to take away someone's freedom or trying to control their every move. While you may feel you're trying to protect her, you're actually just making it worst for yourself.

I've spoken about this in my previous books, but it's so important to spend time apart while in a relationship. You can't insist or expect to spend every free moment by your significant other's side. It's not healthy. You both have to have a social life or all you'll do is depend on another. I'm not saying you shouldn't do activities together; I'm simply saying that spending quality time with friends or family without your partner is okay. You're allowed to live your life. And it's important to function on a day-to-day basis without having to demand your partner's time and attention at all cost.

One of my exes was a possessive jackass. He didn't like me wearing certain things and wouldn't allow me to wear black nail polish, because *he didn't like it* ... but I DID! He would complain if I didn't look a certain way and succeeded several times in lowering my self-esteem.

Many people have been in over possessive relationships and don't realize it until they read about the signs online or in books. Please keep in mind that a little possessiveness is okay especially in situations where you feel desired and they show you that you're the center of their world. But, be very careful with this because that same love and affection can become dangerous if your partner is consistently asking you where you're at, who you're with or gets into a jealous rage because they see you speaking to someone else (a friend, co-worker, opposite sex, etc.) How many times have you heard a friend go through this? Or how many times have you been in that situation, overwhelmed and confused on how to handle it?

The best way to approach this chapter is to list common signs of a possessive relationship so you can compare yourself to them.

1. They control or stalk you.

One of the most obvious signs of a possessive person is when they stalk everything you do. They want to control your every move from where you go to who you're going with to how long you can stay out. They'll demand to know everywhere you go and will even sometimes insist on going with you, because they're afraid you'll cheat on them. That can lead to them insisting on picking you up or insisting on joining you, when you obviously don't want the company.

They'll sometimes even call you to make sure you're with who you said you were going to be with, whether you're with friends or simply running a few errands at the store. Most of the time, they'll get mad because they won't approve what you're wearing or where you're going.

Sometimes, they'll go as far as acting overly protective of you but won't want you to enjoy anything without their company. And that can even lead to a fight in order to make you feel bad for not doing what they wanted you to do. Don't let that be you!

2. They're manipulative and good at it

A possessive person will go out of their way to make you feel as if you're not good enough. They'll lower your self-esteem and will sometimes even make you hate yourself. They'll twist words around to make you feel dumb and will make you feel as if you're not worth it. They'll lower your confidence and make you believe that only they understand you, and they're the only ones who will ever love you. They'll manipulate others around you into believing that they're good to you, while in the meantime treating you like crap when you're alone. Most manipulative people will tell you they "love you" but their actions will prove otherwise.

3. They'll sabotage your relationship with friends and family

This one gets to me because I have several friends that have been through this type of behavior and it's never pleasant to witness people you love going through so much pain.

The moment the possessive person notices you enjoy spending more time with your friends without their presence, they'll hatch a plan to break your friendship up. They'll concoct schemes to make sure you don't spend the same quality time with them and will even lie about them to try to convince you to stop seeing them.

People that are willing to sabotage your relationship with your family because of their insecurities is something to keep an eye out for because they'll say and do whatever it takes to try to pin you against one another. Be careful.

4. They're making all the decisions

Now while it's normal for some people to make decisions, it's not normal for them to make all of them (unless you're into that). If they're consistently making all the decisions and won't let you get a word in, they're overstepping their power. If you disagree with them, it's a cause for an argument and they'll make sure to stick to what they want, even though it may not be what you want.

This type of possessive people are the worst because they'll make sure to tell you what to wear, where to go, when to stay home, etc.

If they start to control your wardrobe, be cautious

because they'll sometimes accuse you of trying to impress others by looking too sexy. They'll make sure you don't wear anything provocative or anything that draws attention because the less you wear, the better for them.

5. They have temper issues

One of the worst signs is when they have temper tantrums over anything and everything. If you do the opposite of what they expect you to do, they'll get mad and might even become abusive. Most abuse happens behind closed doors but that doesn't stop an abuser from doing it in public. Any person that abuses you verbally, mentally or physically needs serious help. It's not your fault if they take out their anger on you but it's important for you to seek help in leaving.

Someone with anger issues will constantly put the blame on you, even though you know you haven't done anything wrong. That person will always make it seem as though they're right and you're wrong. They'll find reasons to argue with you, even if it's because you stayed out too late or spent too much time on the phone with your friends.

Best way to describe this type of person is a

BULLY. They'll blame their behavior on you and will take out their anger on you because it gives them power. The sad reality is they're insecure and they'll do whatever it takes to cover up their truth.

If you happen to see yourself in this specific scenario, I highly suggest seeking help. You may believe you're okay but if you're constantly hurting others with your words or actions, you're clearly not in the right state of mind. The good thing is there are professionals out there that can help and guide you.

Many therapists will gladly work with you towards recovery, but you have to want to get better, or it won't work. The last thing you want is to end up in jail for something that could have been prevented.

6. They won't allow you to have friends of the opposite sex

A possessive person won't agree with you having friends of the opposite sex because they fear you're going to cheat on them, or that you might find a "replacement".
They'll be extremely insecure with this and will

prevent you from seeing them. Some might even contact your friends and tell them to stop calling you or might create fictitious stories to make it sound as if you're mad at them. This is another reason for them to get upset at you over something that is out of your control.

7. They confuse possessiveness with love

No matter what they do to start an argument or if they ever become abusive towards you, they'll always try to turn it around and blame you. They'll profusely tell you that they love you and that whatever they did was out of love... whatever you do, DON'T BELIEVE THOSE LIES. A possessive person will always find a reason to defend themselves, no matter the cost.

They'll scheme and lie, and some will even tell you that they did for your own good. Even when you try to point out their faults, they'll always find a way to manipulate you into believing they did it out of love. You will never be able to change the mind of a person like that because they're caught up in their own world.

They believe that everything they're doing is right even though they're hurting you in the process. THAT'S NOT LOVE.

8. They'll monitor your social media

In this day and age, there are over 2.5 billion people using social media. From Instagram to Facebook to Twitter, there are tons of social media apps out there that can cause any possessive person to monitor your social media activity. A possessive person will stalk your social media day and night. They'll question why your friends with this person and that person. They'll question why you "liked" someone's post. They'll question why you're posting this picture and that picture.

The worst thing that can happen is if they get ahold of your password, they're capable of unfriending people they don't agree you should be friends with. They might go as far as sending messages on your behalf telling lies to get your friends mad at you.

Sometimes, they'll accuse you of cheating on them with celebrities you might be following because they're that insecure with themselves.

They might also accuse you of flirting with random strangers that aren't even on your friends list just because they want to find a reason to start an argument.

No matter how much you try to defend yourself, they'll put the blame on you and might even try forcing you to close your accounts. This might sound unrealistic to some of you, but this does happen every day to many people.

The worst thing you can do is stay in situations like this because you never know what their next steps will be.

CHAPTER 5
Breaking her trust.

"Never make me look *stupid*
while I'm out here being
loyal to you."

- M. Sosa

Men and women are different for several reasons but one thing that has broken many relationships is lying. Once a relationship is compromised, it's hard for the relationship to go back to what it used to. No matter how hard you try, there's an area of the relationship that's been crushed and rebuilding it can take a long time.

You might try to hide the fact that you cheated or lied about something but know that a woman's intuition is dangerous. The moment you think she doesn't know, SHE KNOWS. Men will try to hide things they've done in fear of what their women will say or do, but what men don't realize is that most women will play stupid just to see how far you'll go along with the lie. Once you're caught, get ready because she won't back down and will disclose all the information, she's got on you. She'll throw it all in your face because she knows she's got you in a flat ass lie while you're there trying to convince her that she's wrong. The best thing to do in a situation like this is to come clean, no matter how hard it'll be to say the truth. You won't win this fight but acknowledging that you made a mistake might give you a chance to repairing the relationship.

You've got to understand that a white lie is a no-

no too. Now while you may think there's nothing to it and it won't hurt nobody as long as nobody finds out—a lie is a lie, no matter how small. I get it, your adrenaline is rushing and you're thinking that little lie won't hurt because she won't find out, and if she does, you'll find a way out of it. WRONG! Why would you risk your relationship over something that can be avoided?

This is the difference between a man and woman because women, in general, will think twice before doing something they'll regret while statistics show, men will jump right to the occasion if something excited is presented to them, without blinking twice. In other words, THINK before you do something that you won't be able to get out of or might affect the future of your relationship.

The worst thing you can do is make a woman feel as though she's crazy because you want to protect your lies. I've been in this situation a few times where the man I was dating would sell me sweet lies and make me sound crazy. They would make it sound as if I was imagining the "other" woman or imagining certain situations when I knew I was right.

My mistake was believing them and not trusting my intuition. Their mistake was lying and adding more fuel to the fire to save their asses.

I remember this guy I dated a few years back. Very good looking, seemed to know what he wanted to do in the future, had similar interests as me BUT had too many females around him. Now, while I've never been the jealous type, something didn't add up. He was a trainer and obviously had to interact with his customers but there was something fishy about him. At one point, he connected his cell phone to my laptop and synched his Dropbox account to it. If you don't know what Dropbox is, it's a service where you can sync your phone to this app, and it lets you store a certain number of files in it. Little did he know that every picture he took, came straight to my computer. Any pictures he added to his phone also got stored to my laptop automatically. So, to my surprise, I see a bunch of pictures of one random girl floating around. The funny thing is I had asked him about her a few weeks back because I noticed she kept leaving cute lovey dovey comments under some of his social media pictures. He lied and told me she was his client and the only reason she always put certain comments on his pictures was because she was a regular client. Yet, after seeing those pictures, I confronted him and once again, he lied by calling me crazy and said I was imagining things. Fast forward to a few days later, I decide to message the girl through social media and ask her who she is to him. Come to find out, she's his girlfriend and he's been lying to the both of us for months. To make a long story short, this ass wipe tries to lie to the both of us but can't because he knows he got caught red-handed. He apologizes profusely and at one point, tries to blame me for certain things not going right. Are you fucking serious? Instead of holding himself accountable for the lies he's been spewing to the both of us, he tries to play the damn victim. IDIOT!

When you break a woman's trust, you rock her world to the core. You make her paranoid and suspicious of your every move because she isn't sure what to expect from you. This is why many relationships fail because instead of being honest, it gets shattered with bullshit lies. Trust is critical but once it's gone, it's hard to get back.

You can't expect her to be all smiles and pretend as if nothing happened. That's not how life works. If you messed up, man up. There's nothing more annoying than being surrounded by a liar that doesn't acknowledge his mistakes.

Now you're probably wondering how you get that trust back. It's not that simple. Once trust is broken, most women will try to comprehend why you did what you did and if there's something she could've done differently to prevent you from lying. You have her overthinking why and when things went so wrong. You have her wondering where you are now, who you're with, are you lying again, are you even at work... a million questions flood her mind because all she sees are your lies. She doesn't want to tolerate another disappointment, so she barricades herself behind higher walls that she had originally brought down when she trusted you. See, those walls aren't going to go down any time soon. You're going to have to work hard to show her that you're sorry and that you're willing to make things work.

Your first step is to acknowledge your mistake and own it. Be honest, take responsibility for your behavior. You fucked up. You're human and nobody expects you to be perfect, but you have to take accountability for your indiscretions. Come to term with what you did and how it affected her. Remember, she isn't a puppet that you can play around with however you want. She has feelings and doesn't expect you to be careless with her heart.

Secondly, modify your behavior. Show her that you mean what you say with your actions. Behave in a trustworthy way, consistently. Don't act one way, one day and then act differently another day. That's not going to prove to her that you're trying to fix things. It'll only show her inconsistency and that's the last thing she wants to see.

If you're going to make a change within yourself, dig deep and do what you have to do to modify your behavior. Buying her flowers, chocolates or lavish gifts might work for some but in general, it won't change the fact that she knows you've lied to her. It'll be in the back of her mind until you show her that you're trying to change.

Another step is to put yourself in her shoes. Show her you care and you're aware of what she's going through. Realize what you did and how much it's affected her. Becoming defensive won't help your situation. The truth is out, and deflecting blame isn't going to make things right. It's important you remember that she's in pain and she's going to voice how she feels whether you like it or not. There's no point in making her feel as if she's not supposed to be angry. Once you put yourself in her shoes, you'll realize how it would feel if she had betrayed your trust and did something you wouldn't appreciate. If she's mad, let her yell, let her curse, let her express her pain. This doesn't mean your partner should get violent with you. NOBODY deserves to get attacked. There is no justification for that so if that arises, leave immediately.

It's important your partner understands that they're being understood and especially heard. Validate their feelings and don't shut them out when they are speaking. Remember, you hurt them. You betrayed their trust so it's important to make sure they're doing okay. Display signs of affection and attention. This is crucial in moments like this. It's also crucial for you to explain how your bad behavior affected her. She needs to see that you know you made a mistake and that you're willing to fix it.

Whatever you do, DO NOT PATRONIZE HER. It can be overwhelming and sometimes even traumatizing for someone once they've been hurt. Part of you may feel as though you're not offending her in what you're saying but words like "Yes, I know" or "Okay already" are signs that you're fed up and don't want to hear her anymore. Be careful what you say because some things you'll never be able to take back. Admitting and demonstrating that you care means you're willing to tell her how sorry you are without making her feel as if you're not interested.

Forgiveness is tough after an affair especially when someone else is involved. Getting that trust back will be hard but it's doable if you're willing to put in the work. Having disagreements is normal during a relationship but losing someone's trust can be the end of it if you don't find ways to mend it. Whatever you do, DO NOT make your relationship about the affair or you'll waste valuable years of your life.

CHAPTER 6

Do it now.
Don't procrastinate.

"I told you so many times
what I was feeling, *you just
weren't listening.*"

- M. Sosa

If there's one thing that will upset a woman, it's a man that doesn't make the effort to get things done when he's supposed to. You're probably thinking it's petty or isn't important, but you fail to see how much it bothers her in the long run.

I've been in this situation several times. Perfect examples, I asked one of my exes to throw out the garbage because it was garbage day. I could have done it myself, but I was running late for work and I knew he wasn't working that day. Later in the evening, I come back home to realize the garbage is in the exact same place it was in the morning. He forgot to throw it out because he was too busy playing video games. Are you serious? Or how about the time I asked him to take out the chicken to thaw so it would be ready for the evening, and once again, I come home, and the chicken is still in the damn freezer? Is it pettiness or do I have a reason to get upset?

It doesn't take much to piss a woman off especially when it feels you're doing it on purpose. When she tells you to do something, it's not because she can't do it herself. It's because she's asking you to help her out. Most women nowadays can run everything on their own but when they have someone in their life that they value, and they feel comfortable with you, they'll sometimes ask you to do the smallest things to help.

Sometimes, she's busy caught up doing a million and one things so she asks for your assistance because she hopes you'll get it done. When you fail to do what she asked, it makes her feel as if you're not responsible and as if you don't want to help her out.

Procrastination excuses are the worst especially when it's something that means the world to her. When you find yourself too busy to help her out, you're showing her that she has to do it all by herself. You're making her feel as if she's your slave instead of being your partner. If the tables were turned, do you think she would forget to do the things you asked her to do? Probably not.

You want the woman in your life to trust you. Forgetting little tasks here and there can be your downfall especially if she depends on you to get things done. If you feel it's inconveniencing you, think about how beneficial it will be to your relationship if you do, do it. Part of being in any relationship means you're willing to help one another out. If you can't even do the slightest things, maybe you're in the wrong relationship.

If you don't want to face trouble in the horizon, try to get things done when she asks. I'm not telling you to do everything she asks and obey her ever command. On the contrary, I'm telling you to show her that you care and that you're willing to assist her in times of need. Remember, your job as a man is to protect and show your woman you love her. Doing the smallest tasks show her that you're listening and that you're trying to help her even when you're busy doing other things.

The main point is to TRY. If she's busy cooking, cleaning, doing the laundry and you can't even take the time out to take out the garbage or help her with some of her usual tasks, you're in the wrong relationship. If you're not willing to make the effort to manage your personal activities and balance out your priorities, you're being unfair to her and to yourself. Relationships are about balance. She helps you; you help her in return. That's how you make things work.

CHAPTER 7
You keep talking about your ex

"Your ex is part of your past but all you keep talking about is her. Do you even care that I'm in the same room as you? Do you even realize how much it hurts each time you bring up her name? *Don't do things you wouldn't want done to you.*"

- M. Sosa

When's the right time to stop talking about your ex? That's a tough question to answer because there's no exact timeline for it. Unfortunately for many, the feelings of abandonment or disgust still linger, and they bring those feelings into their next relationship.

While you may feel that talking about your ex won't bother your partner and will help them understand you better, you're wrong. Telling your partner about your previous relationship and all the things that went sour is normal, but it's not normal to keep speaking about your ex whenever an opportunity arises. One of the first steps to moving on with your life is to stop talking about your exes no matter how liberating it may feel. The fact that you're still talking about your ex means you're still giving them attention.

My ex did this to me. He constantly spoke about his ex-girlfriend all the damn time. He kept reminding me how she messed up his credit and how he had trust issues because of her. He spoke about her daily, so it felt like a routine. Every day, like clockwork, he would speak ill about her. It was a constant reminder that she still had a hold on him. She was a third party in our relationship without even knowing it. The fact that he was doing that to me would eventually affect me in my future relationships. I would eventually do the same things to my future partners because I thought it was normal.

And that's exactly what I did a few years later. I was a woman scorned and felt that if my current partner knew what my exes had done to me, he wouldn't think about doing the same thing. I never thought what my partner was feeling because he would sit there and listen to me vent. I probably sounded overdramatic and annoying at some point because it became repetitive.

I was always complaining about the same things my exes had done and how they got away with it. I figured since I was constantly speaking about my exes in a negative manner that my partner wouldn't mind. I only found out how my partner really felt when we were breaking up. He laid everything out on the table and told me how irritating it was to hear me speak about my exes when they were no longer in my life. That's when things hit the fan because I noticed how painful it must've been for my partner to hear me constantly speak about another man that I was supposed to be over.

etimes, speaking about your ex can cause more damage than good. Knowing when to stop is the hard part especially if your partner doesn't communicate how it makes them feel. My motto is simple, don't say things to your partner that you wouldn't want to hear them say back. I wouldn't want to hear my partner constantly speak about his ex unless it was a matter of life and death. I know what she did in the past but the last thing I want to hear is her name in his mouth. Why? There's no point rehashing the past. So, let's leave the past in the past and not bring back situations that will make us both feel a certain way.

It would drive me crazy to hear my partner talk about his ex. All it would do is send me mixed messages on how he really felt about her. Does he still care for her? Does he still want her in his life? Am I not good enough? There's no valid reason to put your partner through that situation unless you're trying to provoke them.

For example, if you tell your woman that your ex was this hot blonde bombshell model from Europe (no matter what negative things you add to it), are you telling her about a formative experience or are you trying to piss her off by making her feel unworthy? You may not realize you're hurting your partner with words because you feel it's an innocent conversation when in reality, you're causing harm to your relationship.

Sometimes, you might feel insecure because your partner is more confident than you. She might be gorgeous and highly intelligent, and since you know she's dated some clever men, you might feel the need to make shallow claims about your exes. It's a way to hurt her and to stroke your ego—DON'T DO IT. You probably didn't mean to make her feel unworthy but saying these things can eventually lead to premature fights and can easily escalate to a breakup.

Whatever you do, if your partner starts talking about their ex, don't do the same back just because you want to be petty. Responding with negative reinforcement is a horrible idea especially if you're planning on keeping this relationship afloat.

The best solution is to communicate with your partner from the get-go. You want to be able to say what's on your mind, but you also don't want to keep reminiscing about the past. Both of you should be able to trust one another enough to speak about things that bother you while at the same time keeping your partner's feelings in mind. Stop talking about memories from the past when you should be working together on building memories in the present.

That is to say, if you're on the other end of the stick and your partner is speaking about her exes all the time, you should understand that she isn't necessarily doing it because she's trying to play head games or trying to upset you (and don't get me wrong, some might be.) You don't know if she's had serious relationship issues that have made her insecure or maybe she's unsure where she is in life now so speaking about her exes is the only way she can find her voice.

Now, while I'm not telling you that you're forced to listen, this is a great opportunity for you to sit down with your partner and speak about the things that bother you. I know it may be irritating to bring things like this to the light, but it's essential you mention it before it gets out of hand.

You're probably wondering how you would do that, right? Pretty simple. Whatever you do, don't cause a commotion. Explain how you feel perplexed because you've noticed her talking about her exes a lot. Mention that you're not upset but you're curious to know why. This is how you start a dialogue and can hopefully get her side of the story. Once you get answers from her, express how that makes you feel. This is crucial because being open in a relationship is important especially if you want to understand one another. If you want to be heard, you have to be willing to listen as well.

Sometimes approaching someone with empathy makes a huge difference in getting an honest answer. Either way, you'll have reached a different level in your relationship because you'll both be working together in finding solutions.

CHAPTER 8
You moved on without letting her mourn the breakup

"You don't owe me an explanation
but moving on doesn't mean
not giving a fuck, *when you really do*."

- M. Sosa

Don't get this situation twisted because you don't need someone's approval after a breakup to move on. But you should be a little more sensitive towards their feelings. That means not showing off as if everything is okay when it probably isn't.

I don't know what goes through a man's mind when a breakup occurs, but I can tell you that statistics show that men move on way faster than a woman does. This doesn't mean they get "over it" as fast, but we'll discuss this a little further down.

When you get your heart broken, the only thing that's keeping you somewhat sane is the hope that the other person is hurting just as much as you. But when you notice they're having the time of their lives through social media or through friends, you question the motive behind it.

The plain truth is most men move on faster but that doesn't necessarily mean they don't feel any emotions. Some just hide their feelings better than others, so it may sometimes feel as if they don't care.

Men, on average, feel less emotional and physical

pain than women after a breakup. It's not because they didn't care or didn't want a future with their partner, it's mainly because women are more selective in their partners and are more invested emotionally. So, when a breakup occurs, it feels like the end of the world. While the man handles the breakup differently because he doesn't know what else to do.

This is a common mistake a man makes after a breakup. They show no remorse or couldn't care less what their ex is going through, so they begin a new venture to let go of their emotions. While a man might feel anger, he's more prone to engage in self-destructive behaviors than women. This pushes men to do things they usually wouldn't do.

Some want to forget the emotions they're feeling by flirting or sleeping with someone new. Having a new body next to you seems like the right strategy to move on but what you fail to see is that you're only hurting the next person and yourself in the process. This isn't constructive at all. Have you thought about how your ex feels, or do you have no compassion whatsoever? This is a destructive way for you to maintain your own self-esteem. And I get it, you're bummed out and you're unsure how to express it.

In previous chapters, I mentioned that men don't always have the necessary tools to deal with their emotions. They were raised to hide their feelings and forced to believe crying is a form of weakness (when it clearly isn't.)

Because of this, many men repress their grieving by faking what they're truly feeling. While some drown their sorrow with liquor, others party it up with their male friends. Others become frightened of intimacy and avoid getting too close to any woman that wants something more. And then there's the ones that will hump anything that moves. They end up going for hookups, pointless booty calls or even revenge sex to try to fill the void. While I understand that a breakup is tough, it doesn't mean you have to self-destruct over it.

And if that's not bad enough, you go and post happy pictures of you and your friends on social media to show your ex you're doing just fine without them. But that's far from the truth because it actually takes men longer to get over a breakup. The fact that you never learned, at an early age, to deal with your emotions, it can sometimes take years or decades to move on.

But you've got to see it from the point of view of a woman too. While she's out crying or overthinking what went wrong, you're trying to heal your pain by inflicting more pain. We feel disrespected and can't understand why you don't feel miserable like we do. So, posting or acting as if you're okay isn't the solution.

Moving on with someone new is the biggest mistake you can make. The fact that you're not fully healed, even if you're attracted to someone new, doesn't mean you should jump into a new relationship. You don't owe your ex anything, but you do owe it to yourself to take the necessary time to heal through every emotion you're feeling. It isn't right for you to jump ship without taking into consideration all the pain you're going to inflict.

When my ex and I broke up, I felt the need to blame myself for everything. I thought I did everything wrong and him ignoring me was a way to punish me for not doing what I should have. Within a couple of weeks, he had women over his house for a party and was living his best life. He drank away his weekends to forget all the bullshit he had put me through. But through it all,

I realized that I wasn't the problem all along—
HE WAS. He wasn't happy with himself. He
couldn't handle being with a woman that was
more confident than him. He felt the need to
lower my self-esteem because he wasn't over his
daddy and mommy issues.

He moved on so fast because he thought he could
forget all the memories we had shared. He
thought moving on with someone new would
spite me (and it worked) but he forgot that it
would eventually hurt him and his new girlfriend
someday. Everything he did to me; he would
eventually do to her.

So, if you ever go through a breakup, remember
that you're not the only one going through the
pain. And while you think moving on within a
few days or weeks is healthy, it isn't. Take the
necessary time to feel what you're feeling fully.
Let it take over and let it all out. Listen to your
feelings. Let go of toxic behavior and take the
time to get to know yourself again. Remember
what it felt like before you were in a relationship.

Remember what it feels like to fall in love with
yourself. Focus your energy on you and don't
take someone else's emotions for granted. Think

before doing something that can cause others stress and pain.

CHAPTER 9
You don't know what you want out of life

"Never feel guilty for things not feeling right.
Settling for something you know in your gut
doesn't feel right is a sign you're lowering
your standards to please someone else.
You know when someone isn't for you.
You know when you're doing something you
shouldn't be doing. You know when deep
down inside, you're not happy. *You know...*"

- M. Sosa

Women want someone who knows what they want out of life, or at least have a plan on how to reach where they want to be. Depending on your age, you should know what you want. If you're in your 20s and you're still trying to figure it out, it's normal but when you're in your mid 30s and you still don't know what you want, there are serious problems that can affect your relationship.

Every time you're indecisive or uncertain, it makes her feel as though you're insecure and fearful of the future. Women want to know that you see them in your future but when you're all over the place, it just places that uncertainty in her head. It makes her question if she's really what you want. This can make or break you.

The last thing you want is for her to feel repulsed by you. She doesn't want a wishy-washy man. She wants a man that takes risks and can make decisions when necessary. It's a turn-off when she can't feel safe around her man. Imagine being with someone who you trust but doesn't have the balls to stand up for himself. Not the type of man she wants to be around. You don't have to have big muscles or be pro-wrestler, but you do have to show that you're not defenceless. She wants to feel that masculine energy from you.

This doesn't mean you're a horrible boyfriend or husband. But it does mean that maybe you need some time away from your relationship to figure things out, or maybe you need her assistance to help you find what you want to do. You need to step up into being the kind of man she can rely on if you want the relationship to work. The same way she makes efforts is the same way you should be doing what's best for the two of you.

When you don't know what you want out of life, you're basically telling her you don't know what you want in your relationship. That can open a lot of issues. When you're unsure what you want, you can't find ways to improve your relationship. You can't offer suggestions or ideas to help it grow. It can also make her question if you even know what your ideal partner is.

Somebody that's unsure what they want out of life might also just settle for something that works for them in the short term. They won't necessarily know what they want long term, so they settle for anything that comes their way. You might stay with someone because you're unsure what a real commitment should look like.

Things like that make her feel uncertain about where your relationship is heading, and she might interpret your uncertainty with not being happy and only staying because she provides you with enough attention and care. That can also make her feel undesired and unfulfilled because she feels she's not helping you achieve your deepest desires. The problem here is your focusing on the wrong things. You're putting off the opportunity of realizing your dreams by becoming passive.

You'll never feel fulfilled in your relationship or in life if you don't communicate and share how to make things better. When you're dissatisfied with yourself, it eventually will create an imbalance in everything you do. And staying in a relationship for the sake of being in a relationship is never going to be a solution to your problems. Now, I'm not telling you to hurry up and figure out what you want out of life. But I am urging you to take the time to seek out what you want out of love and life, and then go straight for it!

CHAPTER 10

You're not satisfying her.

"If you're going to love her,
love her right."

- M. Sosa

One of the reasons a relationship ends is because it loses the spark it once had. At the beginning, things are usually perfect, almost like a fairytale, until time passes by and things start to change.

Back in the days, it was assumed that men were more sexual than women. Nowadays, women are just as sexual than men (maybe more.) But that doesn't mean that you should forget about her needs. The same way you like to get things done is the same way she likes to have her fun too. It's not always about you. Pleasuring her is important even if you think it's not.

Focus on foreplay

One thing many women complain about is the lack of foreplay. She wants intimacy and doesn't mean "wham, bam, thank you ma'am!" The funny part is some men tend to ignore their women's wants because they figure they can go around it and still please them. But that's not always the case. If your woman is complaining about not getting enough foreplay, that's because SHE'S NOT GETTING ENOUGH FOREPLAY. It's not rocket science, if she's telling you that's what she wants, why aren't you making the effort to please her?

Foreplay can be a number of things such as massages, dirty talks, etc. It should be something that excites your partner and sets the mood just right.

Don't get me wrong, having a quickie is fun and exciting but a woman likes to feel desired. If you're always rushing through sex, eventually she'll feel as though she's just a hole. That's never a good sign and can lead to major issues.

Take the time to understand her body. Ask her what she wants and needs. Trust me, what you provide for her will make her explode in excitement. Make her feel special!

Share your fantasies

I understand it can sometimes be frightening to share your sexual fantasies with your woman but once again, communication is important in these situations because you have to know how to express your desires. Many men are afraid to tell their women about their fantasies because they're scared of being judged or mainly scared that their women won't agree to it.

While certain women might be against certain fantasies, others will be willing to do what it takes to please you. But they'll never know if you don't share those intimate secrets with them.

You'd be surprised how many women fantasize about having threesomes or playing with specific toys. Women get bored of the same routine especially if their partner isn't sharing their kinky fantasies with them. You're an adult so why not share your fantasies with her? The worst thing she'll do is decline your invitation on trying new things.

Show emotions

There are women out there that love silent sex, but a greater majority want to hear you moan. They want to know you're into it and don't expect you to be silent.

When you're silent, you're also making her feel as if she's not pleasing you or isn't good enough at what she's going, or maybe you're just not into what she's doing to you. You're not a lifeless doll. Show emotion. If she wanted to have sex with a robot, she would have purchased one. Get the drift? Connect with your woman and that means moaning or looking at her straight in the eyes. You shouldn't lay there lifeless unless you're not into her. If that's the case, you should tell her how you feel and end it. If not, remember that women love to get orgasms too.

CHAPTER 11
She will leave

"The biggest mistake a man can make is believe the woman who's fought so hard to make things work, will never leave. *She will*, and she will give the opportunity to *another man* to cherish what you wouldn't."

- M. Sosa

One of the biggest mistakes a man can make is assume the woman that loves him won't leave. You're wrong. A woman that's fed up will leave for many reasons and it's up to you to stop her.

Let me make this clear. A woman doesn't need you. She wants you to be a part of her life but when you're too busy making her a second priority, she won't hesitate to kick you to the curb or take her things and leave.

She feels alone

A woman wants you to acknowledge she exists. In other words, don't ignore her. When men get too comfortable, they tend to forget the things they used to do. Men detach easily while women are still busy being nurturers. That's why it's so important for you to not forget about her when you're in a relationship.

When you're not emotionally present, you push her further and further away. Eventually, she'll realize that she doesn't deserve to be treated poorly and will walk out of your life. Love and attention are important factors and when they're not reciprocated, you're giving her the green light to leave you.

The same applies to men that put all their attention and main focus into their work. Your office isn't going to keep you company at night or speak with you when you need someone to talk to, right? If you keep putting work first, you might end up losing everything. Know when to take some time off or you'll end up losing valuable time that you could have spent at home instead.

You don't have to give her all your time, because that would be almost impossible. But you can take a few minutes out of the day to listen to one another. It could be during dinner, or right before bed, whatever way you choose will help your relationship. It's understandable that you're busy and you don't have much time but when you commit to something, such as making some time to communicate with one another, it helps in the long run.

You can even leave a little note on her dresser or the fridge that shows your appreciation. It's all about making the smallest gestures to show her that she's not alone.

You don't make her feel sexy

Routine will destroy your relationship because it becomes redundant. She craves your attention because it makes her feel sexy.

Some men will watch porn instead of trying to be spontaneous with their women in the bedroom. What's the point of watching porn alone when you can watch it with your woman? If she's not into that, then maybe sneaking up on her and kissing her gently, seductively will turn her on. Either way, make her feel sexy. Show her that you want her and that she's the only one on your mind.

As a woman gets older, she knows what she wants so when she feels rejected or undesired, she won't hesitate to move on.

You can't see eye to eye

Women, in general, are the driving force to a relationship. They try to find ways to ameliorate communication when things aren't going well. But when two partners can't see eye to eye, it can lead to stubbornness and also lead to splitting up. There is no salvaging a relationship where two people want to be right. It just doesn't work that way. You should be looking to find a resolution by compromising with one another.

When one person thinks they're doing right by the other, the other might think their partner is being selfish and unappreciative. This can cause unrealistic expectations on both sides. One feels they're being taken for granted while the other feels resentful towards their partner. That stubbornness on both ends won't get you nowhere.

The only solution is **communication**. Talk to one another and that doesn't mean nodding your head to everything she says just to make her shut up. This means listening and having an open conversation to avoid any type of resentment from building up. Let it all out. You don't have to agree to everything she says either, but you should make the effort to speak about your frustrations without raising your voice.

Don't bottle your emotions up. Let them be heard. Speak your mind because you don't want to sabotage your wellbeing over something that could have been fixed with a few words. I know it isn't easy to express yourself all the time but its important you listen to what she has to say and it's even more important you express how things are making you feel.

Sugarcoating your issues or trying to hide them under the rug won't fix the problems. If you can't see eye to eye, find a better way to let all the obvious issues out before you reach the breakup stage. Communication is key. What's the worst that can happen? You'll both disagree but at least you'll have tried to rectify the issues.

Her friends listen more than you

One of the reasons women end up leaving loveless relationships is because they find comfort in their friends. If she feels she has a better support group than you, chances are she's strong enough to leave you without thinking twice. It's sometimes easier for women to communicate their dissatisfaction with friends.

This again goes back to communication and why it's so important. Her concerns shouldn't always be discussed with friends. They should be discussed with you first so if she isn't doing that, there's a problem that needs to be addressed. It's nice to have people to talk to but when she feels you aren't listening or aren't taking the time to listen to ask what's going on, you're slowly losing her.

The more she runs to her friends for support, the more likely she is to leave. It's important you find ways to communicate better and make her feel that you are present, so she understands that whenever something happens, she can run to you for help. It's all about that intellectual connection, make sure you don't lose it.

She's fed up

When a woman's fed up, you'll have a hard time convincing her to stay. Women have evolved in today's society and aren't weak minded as they used to be portrayed. They are confident and know when enough is enough.

If you're constantly flirting with other women or doing the opposite of what she asked you to do, or even spending too much money on things you shouldn't be spending them on, you're giving her more ammunition to leave.

Women will tolerate a lot from men but when you're being selfish and inconsiderate towards her feelings, she'll eventually cut you loose. It might not be right away, but it'll build up until she decides to explode. She won't settle for a mediocre relationship that isn't leading anywhere. Men don't always see the warning signs that are staring them right in the face, until it's too late. If she's constantly telling you that something is bothering her, stop doing it. If she's pouring her heart out to you, don't ignore her words. If she's asking you to change your behavior because certain things bother her, try to be more understanding of her needs. She knows her worth and knows that she doesn't have to settle for someone who isn't giving her his half.

It takes a lot for a woman to leave you and sometimes, that's the shakeup you need to get your shit together.

QUOTES

"The moment you meet the right one,
you'll do anything to *protect, provide* and
profess your love to her."

- M. Sosa

"You loved me for all the wrong reasons. You kept taking, taking, taking and I was foolish in love, so I kept giving. You drained me. I lost my self-respect and my dignity trying to make you appreciate and love me. I felt foolish for letting you use me, and dumb for staying for so long when I knew *I deserved better*. Looking back, I'm not longer mad at you. I'm actually happy things turned out the way they did because it taught me to love myself, and also taught me to stop trying to get validation from others. *I'm worthy of love…* I always have been, and that's all I keep repeating to myself."

- M. Sosa

"It was never love.
You don't play head games, constantly lie,
degrade and betray the person you're
supposedly in love with."

- M. Sosa

"The right man or woman will never leave you room to doubt their love."

- M. Sosa

"It's so hard to try to convince a broken person to *trust again*. The scars from their past are sometimes too deep."

- M. Sosa

"Forgiving means letting go
of past mistakes that you've kept
bottled in for too long."

- M. Sosa

"You don't have to be perfect in everything that you do for her. You just have to show her what she means to you by your actions."

- M. Sosa

The brutal truth about breakups and relationships.

Other books by M. Sosa

- The Mistakes of a Woman – Vol 1
- Dilemma: The Quote Book
- The Mistakes of a Woman – Vol 2
- Letting Go: The Quote Book
- Things I Wish I Could've Told Him
- From Heartbreak to Self-Love
- The Mistakes of a Woman – Deluxe Edition
- Moving on isn't easy

All books can be purchased on Amazon, Barnes & Noble, BookDepository and other booksellers worldwide.

Instagram: @sweetzthoughts
Facebook: @sweetzthoughts

The Mistakes of a Man
2018

Printed in Great Britain
by Amazon